Grace Nichols was born and educated in Georgetown, Guyana, but has lived in Britain since 1977 where she now works as a freelance writer. In 1983 she won the Commonwealth Poetry Prize with her first book of poems: *i is a long-memoried woman*. Virago publish her other volumes: *The Fat Black Woman's Poems* (1984), *Lazy Thoughts of a Lazy Woman* (1989) and her first novel, *Whole of a Morning Sky* (1986). Her books for children include two collections of short stories; two books of poems, *Come On Into My Tropical Garden* (1988) and *Give Yourself a Hug* (1994); and anthologies such as: *Poetry Jump Up, Can I Buy a Slice of Sky?* and *A Caribbean Dozen*. Grace Nichols lives in Sussex with her family.

SUNRIS

GRACE NICHOLS

The author acknowledges assistance from
the Arts Council of Great Britain.

A *Virago* Book

First published by Virago Press 1996

A CIP catalogue record for this book is available
from the British Library

ISBN 1 86049 084 0

Typeset in Berkeley by M Rules
Printed and bound in Great Britain by
Clays Ltd, St Ives plc

Virago
A Division of
Little, Brown and Company (UK)
Brettenham House
Lancaster Place
London WC2E 7EN

CONTENTS

Lips of History

Wings

INTRODUCTION

I'm fifteen, leaning through the window of our Princess Street home, having picked up the unmistakable sound of a steelband coming down – the throbbing boom of the bass, the metallic ringing . . . and sure enough two minutes later an open lorry full of steelband men come into being: heads bent over pans, oblivious to everything but keeping the hypnotic pulse of the latest calypso going. Behind them come an ever swelling throng of people, arms linked around necks and waists, a joyous patch-work quilt of bodies dancing or 'tramping' as we called it, under a one o'clock sun shining down in all its inconsiderate glory.

And since I can't bear to be outside such energy, as they move out of sight, I find myself dashing out of the house down the passageway, and onto the streets, pretending not to hear the headmaster-voice of my father shouting from the window behind me, 'Come back here, girl. I say come back.' Who can keep their daughters forever from the 'forbidden' or more 'rowdy-side' of life? With one slip of my hip I manage to make an opening for myself into a wave and am quickly embraced – someone's arm around my waist, another young man's arm around my neck. Thus buoyed and blissed I tramp around the streets of Georgetown in a euphoric rites of passage. That was mini-carnival, Guyana style (usually held on public holidays), a spontaneous chaotic affair that seemed like child's play when compared to the epic proportions of a Trinidad carnival. When I first got my one and only taste of carnival in Trinidad I was six months pregnant at the time and could not follow the bands as much as I would have liked to. Instead I had to watch most of the action sitting in the crowded stalls of the Savannah as band after band, stunning creature after stunning creature: beasts, queens, kings, gigantic flowers, pirates, all went by in an endless flow of colour.

As a child, carnival, steel pan, calypso, in fact anything that came from the ordinary folk including the Creole language itself were despised and regarded as products of a low-class consciousness by the colonial powers that be and by the more snobbish of the upper and middle classes. But despite various repressive measures, which included the banning of the drum, carnival continued to flourish. For as David Cuffy in his article on carnival noted:

Trinidad Carnival is a deeply resonant anniversary from the bondage of colonial slavery; a journey of freedom as well as a mechanism of social release. Its origins escape rigid definitions of history and culture. They encompass European pagan rites, christian festivals, African slavery and the post-emancipation spirit of anger and reclamation.

Integral to carnival are the infectious rhythms of steel drum and calypso. In the same way that poets such as Linton Kwesi Johnson and Jean Binta Breeze have found the rhythms of reggae inspiring, a number of Caribbean poets have found carnival, steel pan and calypso inspiring as well. One thinks of Trinidadian poet Abdul Malik's 'Pan Run', Guyanese writer John Agard's 'Man to Pan' in which he celebrates the steel pan; and in the works of other poets like Derek Walcott, Amryl Johnson, Victor Questel, James Berry, John Lyons . . . I myself have grown up with the words and tunes and rhythms of calypso constantly in my head – sweet calypso with its wit, wordplay, bravado and gusto. It is the music of my childhood through which we got the news and scandals of the day; love and celebration, crime and tragedy, fantasy, politics and philosophy; in fact all of human experience and all in the people's language no matter how 'high sounding'.

One aspect of the calypso that I love is the direct embarrassing and unembarrassing ease with which the calypsonian launches him- or herself into singing about anything, from our 'championness' at cricket to the intruder who invaded the queen's bedroom, nothing escapes the eye of the calypsonian. When singing about sexual matters there is usually *double entendre* and suggestion so that the children can enjoy the calypso at one level while the adults get the deeper meaning. In matters of social injustice or 'battle between the sexes' the calypsonian doesn't mince his or her words. Here is Calypso Rose, one of the few women who've made a successful career from singing calypso, as she assumes the persona of a long-suffering wife who eventually gives her drunken womanising husband his marching orders:

Get out me house, Solomon,
You're a stinking louse, Solomon,
    You are a blight,
    Get out me house,
    Lemme put some light in me life, Solomon . . .

It is generally accepted that calypso has its roots in the African heritage of praisesongs and songs of derision as practiced by the 'professional minstrels' in West Africa. In fact the word 'kaiso', which is used in Trinidad to refer to calypso, has been traced to the African Hausa word meaning 'Bravo'. In 'kaiso' rival artistes would try to outdo each other by oratory rhetoric and wit – aspects that still exist in the calypso tents of modern day Trinidad. I found it interesting however that in an article on calypso by the Trinidadian playright, Errol Hill, the notion was put forward that calypso might have had its source in 'cariso' which was traditionally sung by women. According to him,

> Testimony from old veterans of the nineteenth-century carnival tents, however affirms that the 'cariso' was a woman's song and dance, usually performed in stick-fighting yards as an interlude between the more manly art of duelling with hardwood sticks.

No discussion on calypso, no matter how small, can be made without reference to the greatest calypsonian of all time, 'The Mighty Sparrow', with whom I grew up; from the days of 'Dove and Pigeon' and 'Jean and Dinah' to 'Capitalism Gone Mad' to the spectre of 'Aids'. Whatever his subject, Sparrow puts his finger on the pulse with devastating accuracy and amazingly is still going, combining the arts of folk-poet, musician, raconteur, dramatist, dancer and singer, all rolled into one. In my 'Sunris' poem, a woman makes a journey towards self-discovery and self-naming, through carnival. In this poem I wanted to capture the calypso tone and some of the features associated with calypso – the directness, bravado, rhetoric and 'big word' aspect – but breaking out at times against the more constricting two-line rhyming beat. The woman herself is swept along by the all embracing pulse of carnival, rather like the infectious rhythm of the road-march tune that sets thousands jumping behind it. While being open to the hedonist pull of carnival she's always aware of the 'unknown mission' in mind so that her dance becomes a dialectic, her spree a pilgrimage. In this act of reclaiming herself and the various strands of her heritage she engages with history and mythology and like the calypsonian sometimes resorts to verbal self-inflation to make her voice heard, 'I think this time I go make history'.

At a personal level the word Sunris resonates with the name of my mother, Iris, who like her mythic namesake was for me a 'bridging rainbow'; it incorporates the spirit of Isis and celebrates my own need for the Sun whose golden 'Iris' (though it doesn't come out often) keeps me going in England.

Grace Nichols, Sussex 1996

Slipping the earth-bounders
Who always tried to pin her down
Grabbing at the knees,
She began to dance her own sea-tree
To stretch towards her rainbow raiments,
Rising with the fireflies,
The flickering little stars
That sparked her own divinity.

AGAINST THE PLANET

Red

Red as the colour
I sometime paint my nails,
ten archway windows
in sacramental stain.

Red as hibiscus
and flametree I love,
the brackish red sorrel
that stained me like blood.

That this same red
should be so readily shed,
so easily splattered by butchers
and bombers and childface soldiers.

This red without which
we whiteout forever.

Black

Show me the woman
that would surrender
her little black dress
to a white-robed clan
and I would show you a liar.

Not for their bonfire,
her wardrobe saviour
the number
in which she comes
into her own power.

Go to a funeral
in black and know
that the dead
beside the white candles
will not be offended.

Add amber earrings,
perhaps a hat or scarf of pink
and know you are ready –
for a wedding.
How black absorbs everything.

Stand around at a party
in black – you are your own artist,
your own sensual catalyst,
surprised to say the least
when black brings you

Those sudden inexplicable hostile glances.

White

Never mind how or why –
this slow delight
of waking to a room
that comes out of the
memory of night,
A dusky dawning –
paintings, wardrobe,
hangings . . .

Then walking, a sleepwalker,
holding on to walls of vanilla,
great solid slabs
you could sink your mouth into.
The memories of ancestors,
all that blackness
against whiteness.
The starched religiousness of it.

O I could hold
the globe like a face,
Januslike spinning
from the depths of my dreaming
I could face-up
to the stark white page
already seeded
with the best invisible poem.

Against the Planet

The ones whose
small hands
once played in our blood

Regard us coldly.
But not so cold to go it alone
on the skien of science,

So up they haul us,
irritated as Jesus
was with his earthly mother;

The way her eyes would fall back
from the greatest works
of his heavenly father

To dwell more wonderingly
upon the infant-hymn
peacefully sleeping

In her lap's shadow.
The ten little stars
of his human toes.

Long-Man

(For Barbara Cole who first introduced us to the
Long-Man
For Jan and Tim who came along
And to *The Druid Way* by Philip Carr-Gomm)

On open downland we're as open as he –
Me and Jan, Tim and John,
Kalera and Ayesha,
And the cracked-sun
Has once again withdrawn.
Leaving us to windy shawls
And pewtery greys
To newly mowed down
Fecund-earth which the rains
Had furrowed into clay.

Plod-Plod
Through the caking-blood
Of England's sod,
Our good shoes growing
Sulkier by the minute,
As is my five-year-old,
Whose hand a sixth sense
Tells me to hold,
Despite her intermittent tugging
On this our hill-god pilgrimage.

And even when she manages
To break free, I'm after her,
A wiser Demeter –
Swiftfooted and heavy

13

With apprehension.
Sensing the weald-spirits
In a primitive pull
Of the pagan dimension.

'We're off to see
The Long-Man, the wonderful
Long-Man of Wilmington,'
I sing, humouring her over
The timeless witchery
Of the landscape.

Meanwhile, as always, he's there,
Looming out of the green coombe
Of Windover's womb.

In our heart-searching
And soul-yearning
We come to stand before him,
But soon our luminous eyes
Are nailing him with a
Crucifixion of questions –
Who and Why and How he came to be.
Male, Female, or ancient
Presage of a new androgyny?

With the sun back out
Surely he is benevolent
Corn-God and Shepherd
Of the good harvest?

Sun-in and he's
The Phantom-Symbol
Of all our foreboding.
The Gatekeeper-Reaper
Who would reap us in.
The faceless frozen traveller.
Moongazer.
Green Man-Mirror,
Tricking our eyeballs on –
The cunning chameleon.

But going back over
The wet green swelling
The presumptuous Goddess in me
Looks back and catches him –
Off guard.
Poor wounded man,
The staves in his arms
No barrier to a woman like
She-who-would-break-them
And take him in her arms.

The Dance

(Painting by Paula Rego; Tate Gallery,
London)

Even the white-packed sands
darkened by the shadows
of their dance
is rinsed in blue

Blue nimbus too
over the enigma of faces
the cobbled cliff
the small white moon

Moving to a tune
we'll never know
graceful and solid
in the wind's exposure

How they dance –
simple country folk
come down to take a stand
against the blue sea

And time that will erase their epitaph.

Loveday and Ann

(Two women with a basket of flowers by Frances
Hodgkins 1915; Tate Gallery, London)

One has rolled away –
unwinding in the waves
of her private blue ocean,
knowing how right she is.
The beauty of her smugness –
Not lost on the other who sees
the pleasure of her crabbing-hand
but chooses to stay land-locked,
sulking on the sands of her own
small hurt. While flowers bear witness –
Even in the alcove of friendship
there are distances.

17

The Queen of Sheba replies to Kathleen Jamie

'Scour Scotland for a Solomon . . .'
from 'The Queen of Sheba' by Kathleen Jamie

Dear Kath, here I am lass,
penning these lapis lazuli lines
from the balcony of my spice kingdom,
pausing, every so often,
to watch the birds fly in,
(no longer bringing leaves of cinnamon)
so preoccupied are they these days
with dodging air pollution.

Well, girlfriend, I've just set
my Himyaritic seal of approval
upon your much-loved praise poem.
Indeed, the gorgeous 'hanging baskets'
of my breasts were fitted to a T
not to mention my head, still warm
with memories of the peat,
the bracken; the awestruck lads and lasses.

Having the keys to the National Library
bestowed upon me was such a pleasure
(My love is like a red red rose . . .)
The only wee regret, however,
was that time did not permit
the highland fling, as I've long
harboured a curiosity
about your menfolk's kilts.

But on to more prudent things.
It is with the most cordial
of intentions
for Sheba-Scottish relations,
that I presume to let
my queenly armour slip
revealing some of the nitty-grittier
aspects of my older trip.

Take the shindig in my courtyard
on the morning of our departure –
no less than a hundred cud-chewing
secretly insensed camels
predisposed to wreak a havoc on my buttocks,
simply because I had christened them;
'Ships of the desert'
(I was told this later by their cameleer)

The lavish gifts being loaded for Solomon –
not only gold, myrrh, frankincense,
but also the best of spices;
attendants running around to procure
last-minute dainties; honeycombs, figs, pomegranates.
All my garments perfumed by my favoured gabanum.
Then the great train moving off . . .
to the handbells of musicians.

As you rightly said;
The cool black skin of the bible
could not hold me.
Neither could the Red Sea –
Sand to the left of me; Sand to the right of me

Sand, countless scintillating miles
of it – ahead of me.
The lewd sun pouring down.

I will not go into the nights
of song and dance,
the emblemic music
that pervaded the slyly shifting sands.
Suffice to say
that I was burnished to my ultimate.
It was a fine and stately madness,
but girlgirlgirl Solomon was no mirage.

He was rich where it matters
(And I don't mean his jewelled robes and slippers)
With seven hundred wives –
Edomites, Ammonites, Moabites
(not to mention lovebites)
he would have to be –
behold the half was not told me!
his thighs alone like twin-trunks of the cedar tree.

Well, I came to prove and prove
him I did, with hard questions,
conversing into the most ungodly hours . . .
succumbing slowly to his musk
as he to my gabanum –
two sovereigns shivering
in the heat of love's passions.
So much for wisdom and trade relations.

Well, lass, I must not unbridle
too many memories upon you.
Don't get me wrong, of Solomon I am still fond,
in fact I wrote him many songs
(a bundle of myrrh is my beloved unto me)
but there was no way
I could leave my kingdom
to join a throng.

So our affair did fizzle out
the way these long distance lusts do
when unbacked by the currency
of warm flesh. yet I have no regrets –
ageless, raceless, classless as I am.
Qualities, which incidentally,
should stand us in good stead even as we gird
ourselves for the turbulent winds of the 21st century.

I will stop here. By order of my own royal command.
Regards to everyone in Scotland.

> Yours as ever,
> Makeda, Queen of Sheba,
> High Priestess of Adventure.

The Way Your Sleeping Hand

The way your sleeping hand
still seeks to cup my V-centre
as if it were:

A hand grenade
A briar patch
A goldmine
A worldbank
An agitated fish
A sapodilla
A cosmic calendar
A soft acre

That would somehow
yield enough
to feed the multitude.

Kuan Yin

It was in a Singapore-hot temple
that I first met you, Kuan Yin, meditating
in the inner precincts for our well being.
Mild-eyed. Temperate.
Serene as marble in that climate.

Later, from books I learnt
how once you were banished
to The Temple of the White Bird
Here, despite the pretty name
they assigned you all the arduous
and menial tasks.

But Serpent fetched water for you.
Tiger gathered firewood.
Birds flew back and forth
harvesting the vegetables.
Even Peacock swept the kitchen floor
stunning the boards with the elegant
broom of his tail.

And you perfected yourself.
Life after life,
in pools-of-stillness,
in chants-of-holy-breath,
a calm phoenix.
infuriating the King of Death.

If a lunatic prays to you he is sane.
If one chants the names
of six million buddhas

and another simply says 'Kuan Yin'
both are relieved of their burdens.

So, Mother of the Willow Branch;
Merciful Kuan Yin;
You who sit among us
in the lotus
of perfect enlightenment –

Lead me in

Past Tiannanmen Square,
into these hidden byways
that exist like your eyelids,
rightly lowered to protect you
from the blinding light
of our faith.

The Unknown Word-Soldier

Clutching to his chest
The single arsenal of a book
That is both prayer
And ammunition,

Always he stands before
The neatly shelved infantry.
Always on the frontline
Of his literary territory,

Face giving nothing away.
Our surreptitious stares
Not opening the cranium-gates
To the shadow country of our fear.

Here. In the confines of a library,
All we know for certain
Is that the bookenemies will wilt
Before his silent salute to the word.

Mnemosyne

(Greek Goddess of Memory)

It won't wash with me –
those who say you're a doddery old lady
dispensing bowls of maggoty soup
and mothy memoirs to all and sundry.
An unreliable witness in rose-coloured specs.

Oh no, you're as true as the saltbrine of the sea
to the emotional crystals
not just the dotting of i's and crossing of t's.
The amnesiac, fish trapped in the mirrorless present,
wants nothing but to bring you flooding back –
all the driftwood, salt, lovehates and honey;
Mnemosyne, Memory, Mother of poetry.

LIPS OF HISTORY

Icons

Everything foreign was better than local
Or so it seemed when I was a child,
But perhaps the grown-ups lied –
The shimmering lie
Of the emperor's new clothes.

Among the English icons praised to the skies;
Iceapples, Yardleys, Grapes,
The unseen Snowflake.
We'd watch the shopkeeper's crafty hands
Among the apple-crates.

The way he'd carefully
Pull back the crinkled tissue
As if it was cotton-wool
And the glistening red unbittens,
Jewels instead of fruit.

On Christmas morning if we were lucky
We'd delve deep to find an apple-ruby,
Our stocking's only bit of edible magic.
Who knows why I was hardly ever tempted
To bite or ravish.

Even now in England's supermarkets
I instinctively leave
The polished red, going instead,
For the common locals –
Cox's orange-pippins, Russetts.

Still I must say that it gladdens the heart
To see how both my apple-eating daughters
Have emerged; carefully avoiding the pith and pips,
While drooling endlessly over the mango
Two sun-starved Eves –

Making a meal of the old creation myth.

First Generation Monologue

Like every other Caribbean emigré
who'd put away the lamp of the sun
She spoke of the bad old migrant days:
I was in the ship's first wave.
No, I never realise it would have been
so cold and grey, so damp and dull
with all the buildings looking like
a prison-front, and even the dwelling
houses excluding my woman's walk;
the closed-up open shops. The fog.

Yes, it seemed as if the whole of England
was a Scrooge in those days of
four-people-living-in-a-room.
The smell of clothes, dank,
before the only heater.
The white landlady exact as the coin
clanking in the grudging meter.

I never forget the night
I got the news how Cousin Bernice negligée
catch fire while warming her foot
in front the parafin heater on the floor;
how she run outside screaming into the cold:
Lord, Lord, to come all the way
to England, Bernice, a bright brown moth
just flickering out on the snow.

*

Still I lighted my days
with memories blue as the indigo
of my mother's rinsing water.

31

I lighted on my memories
like a grasshopper.
Sometimes I was as stranded
as a salmon,
holding my fading hands
before the English fire.
How I longed for the openness of verandahs.

*

Eternity was greyness to me, I tell you,
the days I dragged myself across the days,
barely managing, snail-like
under that amorphous octopus of a sky.
The days I got my colours mixed –
a dream of colours –
on my brain's muddled palette;
Bright blue suddenly brushing grey aside,
slate-roofs glinting galvanise
and everywhere the shimmering
waves of heat,
Evergreens dripping
redblood blossoms at my feet.

*

Europe had become
part of my possession,
but how to come to terms
with the architecture?
The walls sealed and solid;
The closed door against the cold;
The ivy of my voice no longer
climbing towards the ceiling –
To overhang green and listening.

*

Where were my days
of leaning through windows.

parting the Trades?
Breezing out with Bo
in the shade of the backsteps,
dress lapped between legs like a river.
Loud ice in lemonade.
Bird-picked mangoes hiding in foliage.
Fowls grazing the backyard,
clean-neck, feather-neck,
each solitary,
eyes pulled down –
little photographic hoods
from the glare of the sun.
And Hibiscus, queen of all the flowers,
cupped red and rude against the paling,
still glistening with little mercuries
from the earlier shower of earthsmelling rain.
But never enough to keep us rooted.

Hurricane Hits England

It took a hurricane, to bring her closer
To the landscape
Half the night she lay awake,
The howling ship of the wind,
Its gathering rage,
Like some dark ancestral spectre,
Fearful and reassuring:

Talk to me Huracan
Talk to me Oya
Talk to me Shango
And Hattie,
My sweeping, back-home cousin.

Tell me why you visit
An English coast?
What is the meaning
Of old tongues
Reaping havoc
In new places?

The blinding illumination,
Even as you short-
Circuit us
Into further darkness?

What is the meaning of trees
Falling heavy as whales
Their crusted roots
Their cratered graves?

O why is my heart unchained?

Tropical Oya of the Weather,
I am aligning myself to you,
I am following the movement of your winds,
I am riding the mystery of your storm.

Ah, sweet mystery,
Come to break the frozen lake in me,
Shaking the foundations of the very trees
within me,
Come to let me know
That the earth is the earth is the earth.

High-Tea

High-tea with white wine
and I conversing
with the 'best of dem'
hightalk for hightalk
literati for literati

Shakespeare
Milton
Keats
Shelly

Walcott
Brathwaite
Miss Lou
Berry

Daffodils
Sonnets
Quartets
Laureates

Hibiscuses
Odyssies
Trilogies
Prophets

Until flushed with wine
and too much articulation
I decide to sit down
rattling the teacups
of the Anglo-Saxon tradition

But what is this nice
pink-cheek
old-chap
saying beside me?

He wants to valet me
bring me up newspapers
cups of tea
pull back curtains
clean my shoes
and bathe my feet
like he did some
Argentinian Mistress
long deceased.

Symbolism
Surrealism
Imagism
Fetishism

High-tea
or
Low-tea
among the literati.

Berlin Snapshots

I

The unbelievable
green trees
of Mayakovskiring,
Regimentally lining.
Tree-soldiers
helmeted in their
own leafy spreading.

Daring to be buoyant with the wind.

II

An old East German man
standing at a gate
in this one-time
Jewish residential area,
bewildered as a ghost
thrown from the walls
of an obdurate era.

III

Tacheles

The battered backface
of a building's façade,
peeling and graffitied
like an idea of da Vinci
stripped down;

A stage set with
iron props and masks –
the rusting memorabilia
of some phantom opera
twisted and dark;

An old tank lockjawed;

A metal tree –
tube tip yearning
to blossom into filigree.

IV

Sitting in a Turkish cafe
once bunker, with Bettina,
raising the bowls of steamy
milky coffee like orientals
to our lips.
Seduced by bright cushions
and an air of homeliness
I sing her 'Little Red Bird
In Your Cage Of Ribs'
from Walcott's *Joker of Seville*,
(She's doing a thesis on him).
Bettina and her sweet inimitable smile,
Bettina and her innocently cropped blond hair,
The Führer's furious shadow
following us back up the stairs.

V

And Michael still rides,
dark and vulnerable into the night,
despite the beating that left him hospitalised;
Europe's African child,
cycling off with a philosophical grin.
Can't decide whether he loves or hates Berlin.

VI

Everywhere ghosts
of the old military.
Everywhere kisses
from the thick lips of history.

My Northern-Sister

(For the Finnish-Swedish poet, Edith Södergran, 1892–1923; who
kept faith in her words despite the critics)

Refusing the crown that would wreathe her as dumb,
my Northern-Sister comes, saying, 'It does not
become me to make myself less than I am.'

And she moves into forest
and she brings me out handfuls of snow,
a rugged fir,
a taste of wild thyme,
which is only a taste of her own joyousness –
the fearless gates she keeps open,
including the one for death.

And she gives me heather and pine,
a taste of blue air,
the talking-memory of my own childhood trees,

Weaving a tender chemistry with her red
red heart.

And what have I got to give her?
Only the little thing she says
she's always wanted –
a small letter, to be read on a garden bench
with a cat in the sun.

Edith, my sister, come and sit down.

At the Bottom of the Garden

No, it isn't an old football
grown all shrunken and prickly
because it was left out so long
at the bottom of the garden.

It's only Hedgehog
who, when she thinks I'm not looking,
unballs herself to move –
Like bristling black lightning.

Timehri Airport to Georgetown

Coming down, from Timehri
To Georgetown,
Earth knitted in broader patches
Of a tighter green.

Echoing pull of forest,
Ominous call of jungle.
Road shimmering like waves
Of aluminium in the mid-day heat.

Smell of earth
Through the half open
Airport taxi window,
That and breeze, stiflingly welcome me.

Eyes pinned open
To watermelon, watercoconuts,
Huge papaws dangling like
Bright heavy lanterns from roadside stalls.

Mangoes, drop-pearl stems
I'd almost forgotten,
The splayed dicotyledonous
Of breadfruit leaf.

And coconut tree
Standing like modest intercedary,
Between earth and sky,
Between sky and sea.

The hub of branches –
The long veined leaves,
A supplicant-spider,
Spinning a prayer in its weave.

Blackout

Blackout is endemic to the land.
People have grown sixthsense
and sonic ways, like bats,
emerging out of the shadows
into the light of their own flesh.

But the car headlamps coming towards us
make it seem we're in some thirdworld movie,
throwing up potholes and houses exaggeratedly,
the fresh white painted and grey ramshackle
blending into snug relief.

And inside, the children are still hovering,
hopeful moths around the flickerless Box
immune to the cloying stench of toilets
that can't be flushed. The children,
all waiting on electric-spell to come
and trigger a movie, the one featuring America,
played out endlessly in their heads.

While back outside, coconut vendors decapitate
the night, husky heads cutlassed off
in the medieval glow of bottle lamps.

And everywhere there are flittings
and things coming into being,
in a night where footfall is an act of faith –
A group of young girls huddled in a questionable
doorway;
The sudden dim horizontal of an alleyway;

And the occasional generator-lit big house,
obscenely bright –
hurting the soft iris of darkness
in this worn-out movie, slow reeling

Under the endless cinema of the skies.

On the Eve of the Summer Solstice

(In Brazil, thousands come down to the seaside to
pay homage to this Goddess who accompanied them
from Africa to the new world more than two
centuries ago)

Flowers cast
on the bosom
of ocean

For you, Yemanja,
for you

Lighted candles
set sail
on rafts

For you, Yemanja,
for you

Tributes and triunes
from canoes
robes of cool colours

For you, Yemanja,
for you

For you who still rock us,
little fishes,
in the cradle of your ocean

For you to whom we bring

our burdens
like dirty bundles of washing

For you who slap and beat us
who blue and rinse us
who leave us

O so much lighter to dry.

To the Running of My River

(For Kamal)

Sound the tabla and the sitar!
Pile high my banks
With fruits and flowers –

Here comes my unsaried daughter
Walking in the simple
Creolisation of herself.

But mark well –
In the black swing of her hair
She is still potential possessee of Kali,

In the dusk of her eye
She still keep faith with Diwali,
This daughter whose ricegrains

Swell with prosperity even as she moves
In full knowledge of the hard
Ships of her immigrant history.

Listen. To the tremor of India,
Still residing
At the bottom of her every speech.

SUNRIS

Carnival is all that is claimed for it.
It is exultation of the mass will,
its hedonism is so sacred, that to withdraw
from it, not to jump up, to be contemplative
outside of its frenzy is a heresy . . .

DEREK WALCOTT

If you hear she Fire, Fire,
In meh wire, wire,
Ay, ay, ay, oy, oy, oy,
Fire, Fire, Benaca me pito
Damay mucho agua, heat for so . . .

CALYPSO ROSE

SUNRIS

Out of the foreday morning –
They coming
Out of the little houses
Clinging to the hillside –
They coming
Out of the big house and the hovel –
They coming
To fill up like mist dis Jour Ouvert morning
To lift up dis city to the sun
To incarnate their own carnation.

Symbol of the emancipated woman I come
I don't care which one frown
From the depths of the unconscious I come
I come out to play – Mas Woman.

This mas I put on is not to hide me
This mas I put on is visionary –
A combination of the sightful sun
A bellyband with all my strands
A plume of scarlet ibis
A branch-of-hope and a snake in mih fist
Join me in dis pilgrimage
This spree that look like sacrilege.

But those who cannot see
Into the intricacies of my blood
better watch they don't put
They foot in they mouth,
Aspersions cast of race
Will not ricochet
But will sink into
The objection pores
Of my every bone, for;

      I'm a hybrid-dreamer
      An ancestral-believer
      A blood-reveller
      Who worship at the house of love.

So Coolieman, Blackman, Redman come,
Potageeman, Chineyman, Whiteman, Brown,
Whoever throw they hand round mih waist
I come out to tasteup mih race
But when I ready I moving free
I sticking to the flight of my own trajectory
I reaping the flowers of this deep dance mystery
I think this time I go make history.

Hands Hands
Is all a matter of hands
Through the shaping and the cutting
Through the stitching and the touching
Through the bright door of love
Come the splendour of hands.

> *And is dih whole island*
> *Awash in a deep seasound*
> *Is hummingbird possession*
> *Taking flight from dih ground*
> *Is blood beating*
> *And spirit moving free*
> *Is promiscuous wine*
> *Is sanctity.*

Feet Feet
Is all a matter of feet
For the spirits
Take entry from the feet
High-priestess and Devil
Aztec-King and me
Midnight-robber, Saint Theresa,
And Jab-Jab Molassi,
All carried by
        The-rise-and-fall
        The-rise-and-fall
The tranced unstoppable rhythm
And Death mingling free
In his white wing-beats
We ain't stopping
Till Ash Wednesday
Put a kick in we heels.

But O Montezuma,
How could you deliver all the glory
Without a fight?
Gold, you had enough to bribe all heaven,
Paving a haven for our souls.
From the mouth of the Yucatan,
Man, the whole Caribbean.

Montezuma:

Woman, hush your mouth,
Who among us would not have been beguiled?
All the ominous omens and the signs –
A volcano's eruption
The waters of Lake Texaco's rise
A comet sitting like a photograph
No, it was written
In the invisible ink of legend
Across the ageless parchment of the skies.
Feathered-Serpent, Plumed-God,
It was always known that the Great
Quetzalcoatl
Would return to claim his own.

But the radiance, Montezuma,
The shattered radiance –
Toltec, Olmec, Zapotec, Aztec . . .
No, you can't licence my polysyllabic tongue
All your temples, codices, Tenochtitlan . . . gone.

Montezuma:

Woman, blame the messengers who run
Their relaying marathon.
Blame the fear hammering in their chests
And the picture of that –
Half-horse, half-man God
Which they transmitted to my breast
Blame the fools bringing me news
Of him who was only Cortez.

I remember it as if I was there,
Montezuma, watching transfixed,
It was as if, legend made flesh
Had descended out of the clouds and mist.
I remember how you tried to woo a return
Sending forth gifts –
A hoop of gold as big as a cartwheel
With engravings of the sun;
A smaller one in silver to signify the moon;
Statues of ocelot, birds, all wrought in gold
You din expect them to turn back . . .

                              those conquistadors?

Montezuma:

Woman, blame the bible and the sword,
Blame that cross of a blood-devouring sun
Look, just blame the fatalist
Sitting on the throne of my own heart,
Woman.

And is dih whole island
Awash in a deep seasound
Is hummingbird possession
Taking flight from dih ground
Is blood beating
And spirit moving free
Is promiscuous wine
Is sanctity.

Streets Streets
Is all a matter of streets
Streets perspire freely
Streets arch back ever so slyly
Streets pulsate
In the deepest centre
Of their asphalt selves
Wave after wave –
Streets shudder and groan;
'Gimmie all the weight and the glory
Fill and trample me
colour and stretch me . . .
                              to infinity

O motion in art
Look art in motion
If is not . . .
Kanaima and he deathcrew
riding the ocean!

A band of skeletons
With knives in they sides
A mincing apparition
In a menacing sway
Pushing me kinetically
Out of the way
But the road make to walk
On carnival day.

Well if life is a dream
Then I is a dreamer
If is not Papa Bois himself –
The old deer-footed, leaf-bearded curator!
Coming down in a canopy of forest-cool light
Keeper of the green cathedral
(I best be polite)

'Bonjour, Buenos dias,
Good day, Papa Bois,
How the caretaking coming, Sir?'

But the Guardian of the heartland
Barely knowledges the greeting
Brushes an invisible tree-web
Glances upward at his swaying leafy ceiling
Like he intent only on the prayerful breathing
Even in the sea of all this heaving weaving
                              sunhot spreeing.

Pour rum
Beat gong
Steel drum

      On fire

Rhythm sweet
Blood hot
Don't stop

      On fire

O hip roam
Dance foam
River comb

      On fire

Jump higher
Jump higher

Father forgive us for we know not,
Forgive the man who just place he hand
on my promiseland
Later he will take the ash and close he eye;
Man born of woman, you born to die.
Spirit preserve my harvest
from their Fat-Tuesday eyes.

Among wings am I
Angels, imps, devil-kings,
Icarus still battling to
Take off in the wind.
Among labyrinth of sounds
Galleries of colour,
It was me of my own free will
Who choose to be embraced by this river.
To enter freely into this sweat-of-arms
Wrapped like innocent electrical eels about me
No, nobody tell me it would be easy –
                    The rapturous rapids and pitfalls
                                        of this journey.

But, but . . . Miracle of vision!
who is dis woman in a shroud of grey
making the dancesteps of mourning
even as she clears a space for her way?
    Moving like a river whose source cannot be found;
    If is not Africa herself
    lost in the ripples of her own dimension . . .

Africa? How to begin
after all this time and water?
I must begin by telling you
that your presence have endured
despite all the dark-despising
and death-dooming spread about you.
How dih governors-of-art tried to tear
every ounce of civilisation from your heart
even as they basked in the relief
of your darkness
laying all their enlightened fears
at dih gateway of your forest.
Even as they seeked to reduce you, their host,
to a footnote in their notes.

But you know more than me
That spirit must return to spirit
That darkness is a concentration of light
That no one can put a knife
Between the sun and the night
So you endure – spinxlike
In the desert you endure
Knowing it's only a matter of time.

Africa, whenever I remember my father
soberly pouring a small libation in a corner
or my mother rounding fufu in her mortar
The simple burial of a navelstring –
I think of you too and I marvel
how your myriad rituals
have survived the crucible.
How they remain with us like relics
        in the pillow of our unconscious . . .

Africa:

'History is a river
That flow to the sea
Laced with the bone of memory
Ride high her choreography
Pay homage in ceremony'

Yes, I rippling to the music,
I slipping past the old ship,
watching symbol of ship
turn symbol of flowering tree
as if imagination
if the only hope for reality.

And is dih whole island
Awash in a deep seasound
Is hummingbird possession
Taking flight from dih ground
Is blood beating
And spirit moving free
Is promiscuous wine
Is sanctity.

How hammer blows
Can make such sweet tones
How doves can rise
From steel throat
Will always be
A mystery to me.

Underbelly pan
with dih innerbelly
stars
of the underbelly
people
let dih filaments
of your overbelly
sounds
pitch a filter
through blue crest
of old pirate water.

Spread re-echo
regather
down down
wake dih ear
of the middle passage
drown.

Speak to the
Sauteur leap
even as you sweeten
the bones of our
indigenous one's sleep.

Spread, re-echo
re-gather
round round
touch ground
of Atlantic
brown.

Scatter
like minnows
the shadows
of Jonestown

Underbelly pan
with dih innerbelly
stars
of the underbelly
people
pierce us with
yuh holy steel
make your octaves
to fall on us
like a benediction
of leaves.

Blessed is the first cool shadow of darkness
Blessed is the deep well of our language
Blessed is the space that the spirit inhabit
Blessed is the robe we reserve for it
Blessed is the need of our communion
Blessed is the fire of our consecration.

An is so dih trade winds
urging me with hands of jubilation.
An is so dih trade winds
fanning me with hands of rejuvenation.

An is so I coming in
to dih carnival straights.
Is that Legba playing cripple
by dih crossgates?

Bless my eyesight
Is a whole heap of deity
like they come out to greet me
I think dis time I go make history.

Columbus, you is not the only one
who can make discovery.

Heipya Oya in your red and purple gown
strike me a light, sweet power woman

Beat dih iron Ogun
lemme hear dih metal ring
Boom dih bass out Shango
Dih crowd they thundering

Cool me down Yemanja
bathe my face in your river.
Dance yuh dance Kali
destroy, renew me with each blood-shiver

I recognise you by your head-dress
O Makonima

And you too Virgin Mary gyal
shaking up like celebration
I see dih Pope casting doubts
bout your immaculate conception

Iris, Iris, you arcing before me
in a rainbow bridge
Isis, Isis, quintessential one of Egypt
what is that word you waving at me like a script?

Dih characters seem familiar
but I can't quite remember it . . .

O symbol of the emancipated woman, I come
I don't believe I see one frown
From dih depths of dih unconscious, I come
I come out to play Mas-Woman.

Dis mas I put on is not to hide me
Dis mas I put on is visionary,
A combination of the sightful sun
A belly-band with all my strands
A plume of scarlet ibis
A branch of hope and a snake
In my fist.

With the Gods as my judge
And dih people my witness,
Heritage just reach out
And give me one kiss.
From dih depths of dih unconscious
I hear dih snake hiss,
I just done christen myself, SUNRIS.

WINGS

Wings

(For John Figueroa, Jamaican poet

Inspired by his comment that as Caribbean
people we're preoccupied with Roots, when
maybe we should be signifying ourselves by
Wings – 'Out of the Margins Festival', South
Bank, London 1993)

Consigned to earth
we thought it fitting
to worship only
the sustenance of our roots,
so that when uprootment came
in its many guises
we moved around like
bereaving trees, constantly touching
our sawn-off places.

And though we pretended to be
bright migrant birds
it was always an inward yearning
for the compelling earth
of our roots – lost Africas, Indias,
then the love-tugging land
of our immediate birthmothers.
Past more poignant
than any future.

Root-lovers
Root-grounders
Root-worshippers,
We've been

old hoarding mourners,
constantly counting
our sea-chest of losses,
forgetting the other end
of our green extremis –
the imperishable gift of our wings.

But wasn't it wings
that made our ancestors
climb the airy staircase
whenever they contemplated
rock and a hard place?

And isn't it wings, our own wilful wings,
still taking us into migratory-pull
still taking us into homing-instinct,
beating up the winds
to find our respective heavens?

And even if we stay
blissfully or unblissfully still,
in sun-eye or snowflake-kiss
it's still wings taking us back
to the bigger presence of wings.

Wings over women
beating clothes on stones
resting faith on river-water
and the soapless transfiguration
of clothes.

Wings over my sacred village road,
dust bringing sandflies,
candleflies

and Jordanites,
dark as their robes were white,
religious man-moths, hobnobbing
around scriptures by gaslight.

Wings over my mother
who leaned on light
who could make a meal
from love alone in no time.

Wings over the unpainted little shack
of my nextdoor neighbour,
shaking with music and laughter
on the christening of his baby daughter,
the amplifiers and loudspeaker
he's erected outside, proclaiming him King,
everything threatening to take off
in tradewind.

Wings over my hardpressed sister,
who, when I went back home,
flew around, gathering a get-together,
a flocking of family, friends, neighbours,
food, singing, all determined
to send me (wet-eyed grateful sinner)
flying high 'wid dih gift of dih holy fire'

And wings over you, John,
for your white-bearded
and timely reminder
of our wings.

Oasis

Intersections of the sun
I'm the ancient one

The hierographee
On the rock

I'm the one that
Binds the blood

The one who sets out
For the desert

While the rain-maker
Does his dance

When it comes to water
I never trust to chance.

GLOSSARY

Iris: Greek goddess of the rainbow and natural peace-maker. In many mythologies, she personified the bridge between earth and heaven.

Isis: Egyptian goddess, wife of Osiris and mother of Horus, she became one of the most important deities in the Mediterranean world and in the Roman empire. Usually depicted in the head-dress of a solar disc and the horns of a cow, she is known as the Mistress of Magic and Speaker of Spells who obtained the secret name of the God Re or Ra.

Kali: 'Dark Mother' is the Hindu Goddess of destruction, creation and preservation. Although in the West she is commonly known in her destroyer aspect, her spiritual significance lies in the belief that she confronts and frees us from our worst fears.

Kanaima: Amerindian figure of death. Also the spirit of vengeance.

Kuan Yin: Best loved of all the gods and goddesses in Chinese mythology as well as in the rest of the orient. She is the chief symbol of compassion, peace and generosity.

Long-Man: Reclining on the hills of the Southdown (halfway between Lewes and Eastbourne) is the mysterious figure of the Long-Man of Wilmington. Like the Cerne Giant in Dorset, he is carved out on the Chalky hillside, reaching a height of 231 feet. He is said to be the second tallest of such figures in the world, the first being the giant of Atacama who stands at 393 feet high on the side of the Sierra Unica mountain in northern Chile. The Long-Man, or Green Man, of Wilmington continues to mystify generations of visitors and there is still much speculation as to whether he was carved out by the monks from the Wilmington Priory in the Middle Ages. Whether he is Saxon, Celtic or even Roman in origin, he remains naked, featureless and enigmatic. The silent figure of the Long-Man with his two staves invites us to solve the mystery. (For further reading see *The Wilmington Giant (The quest for a lost myth)* by Rodney Castleden.)

Makonaima: The Great Spirit of many Amerindian tribes, similar in importance to Jehovah.

Montezuma: He was the Aztec emperor or king in power at the time of the arrival of the Spanish conquistadors in the early sixteenth century. Through a series of bizarre coincidences, Cortes, leader of the Spanish invaders was looked upon as the returning God, Quetzalcoatl, come back as legend had predicted, to claim his kingdom. The Aztec priests in the temples had foretold of his coming. Quetzalcoatl whose name meant 'Feathered Serpent' was said to have come down from heaven (long before anyone could remember) in the form of a priest-king. He ruled for a while but was driven out by the old tribal God, Tezcatlipoca. Quetzalcoatl was said to have boarded a magnificent raft and made the prophecy 'I will return in Ce Acatl (One Reed Year) and re-establish my rule. It will be a time of great tribulation for the people.' He then disappeared towards the East. The priests described him as having white skin and full beard and claimed that he would be wearing black upon his return.

Amazingly Cortes landed in Mexico (Vera Cruza) in the year 1519, a one Reed Year on the Aztec calendar. He was wearing black because it was Good Friday; he was white and had a beard. The messengers who relayed the news to Montezuma also described the 'strange terrifying beasts that the invaders had brought over. For the smooth brown-skinned Indians it was their first encounter with the horse and with the Europeans.

Montezuma, already agitated by a series of events which he saw as ill omens (including the appearance of a comet and the eruption of a volcano), sent forth glorious gifts to Cortes, thinking that perhaps this 'God' would be pacified and return to the East. But this only wetted the appetite of the conquistadors and what eventually ensued was the destruction of that whole civilization. (For further reading see *The Caribbean People* by Lennox Honychurch; Nelson Caribbean.)

Papa Bois: Caribbean folk figure. The old man of the woods. A Pan-like cloven-footed custodian of the forest who objects to its wanton destruction.

Legba, Ogun, Oya, Shango, Yemanja: Are all part of the Yoruba pantheon of gods and goddesses in West Africa.
Legba: The guardian of the crossroads and of the sacred gateway. He is prayed to, to open up the realms of possibility.
Ogun: God of war. Symbols include the knife, iron and anvil. He is the father of metamorphosis; the patron of those who work in metal, wood and leather.
Oya: Goddess of the wind, she represents sweeping

change. One of her major symbols is the mask.

Shango: God of lightning and thunder. Represents male fertility. His most common symbol is the double-edged axe.

Yemanja: The ultimate symbol of motherhood. Orisha of the river and the ocean. She is said to have attained greater proportions since her 'middle passage' crossing to the New World and is widely worshipped, especially in Brazil.

LAZY THOUGHTS OF
A LAZY WOMAN

Grace Nichols

'Grace Nichols is a talented poet, and her skill with language is most apparent' – **City Limits**

In this sensuous, witty and provocative new collection are poems of laid-back and not-so-laid-back musings, sagas and spells, thoughts on greasy kitchens and patriarchal theology, bikinis and Caribbean migration. But there are moments of poignancy and loss too – as Grace Nichols takes us through the restless, quirky celebration of her own imagination.

THE FAT BLACK WOMAN'S POEMS

Grace Nichols

'Not only rich music, an easy lyricism, but also grit and earthy honesty, a willingness to be vulnerable and clean' – **Gwendolyn Brooks**

Grace Nichols gives us images that stare us straight in the eye, images of joy, challenge, accusation. Her 'fat black woman' is brash; rejoices in herself; poses awkward questions to politicians, rulers, suitors, to a white world that still turns its back. In the other sequences of this collection, Grace Nichols writes in a language that is wonderfully vivid yet economical of the pleasures and sadnesses of memory, of loving, of 'the power to be what I am, a woman, charting my own futures'.

WHOLE OF A MORNING SKY

Grace Nichols

'She has the discipline of a poet; there are no wasted words or excessive descriptions, but a sure sense of what is sufficient . . . Nichols has wit, acidity, tenderness, any number of gifts at her disposal'
– **Jeanette Winterson**

Along with the sweep of political upheavals – strikes, riots, and racial clashes – daily life in the Walcotts' Charlestown neighbourhood and beyond gathers its own intensity. Tension peaks in the neighbourhood one terrible night when the Ramsammy's rum shop is threatened with burning. Archie, troubled by the times, tries to keep a tight rein on his family. And young Gem, ever watchful, responds with wonderment and curiosity to the new life around her. In this her first adult novel, Grace Nichols richly and imaginatively evokes a world that was part of her own Guyanese childhood.

☐	Lazy Thoughts of a Lazy Woman	Grace Nichols	£5.99
☐	The Fat Black Woman's Poems	Grace Nichols	£4.99
☐	Whole of a Morning Sky	Grace Nichols	£6.99
☐	The Complete Collected Poems	Maya Angelou	£9.99
☐	We, the Dangerous	Janice Marikitani	£8.99
☐	Lyrical Campaigner	June Jordan	£5.99
☐	Rotten Pomerack	Merle Collins	£8.99

Virago now offers an exciting range of quality titles by both established and new authors which can be ordered from the following address:

Little, Brown and Company (UK),
P.O. Box 11,
Falmouth,
Cornwall TR10 9EN.

Fax No: 01326 317444.
Telephone No: 01326 317200
E-mail: books@barni.avel.co.uk

Payments can be made as follows: cheque, postal order (payable to Little, Brown and Company) or by credit cards, Visa/Access. Do not send cash or currency. UK customers and B.F.P.O. please allow £1.00 for postage and packing for the first book, plus 50p for the second book, plus 30p for each additional book up to a maximum charge of £3.00 (7 books plus).

Overseas customers including Ireland, please allow £2.00 for the first book plus £1.00 for the second book, plus 50p for each additional book.

NAME (Block Letters) ....

....

ADDRESS ..../..

....

....

☐ I enclose my remittance for ....

☐ I wish to pay by Access/Visa Card

Number ☐☐☐☐☐☐☐☐☐☐☐☐☐☐☐☐

Card Expiry Date ☐☐☐☐